Mirage

Edition-1

By <u>Aavriti Vikash</u>

<u>The BOOK</u>

This book is a collection of quotations that helps us navigate the challenging times in life – by people who have been there, done that and lived to let us know the wisdom 😊

"Life would be tragic if it weren't funny", Stephen Hawking.

with this collection of quotes by inspiring leaders, sketches that inspired me and a few of my paintings, let's start the journey together of bringing hope, seeing positives, and surrounding ourselves with love, luck, and laughter.

I dedicate this book to all of You, hoping these pages help you find your passion, perseverance, and strength. Let's keep smiling together.

— Aavriti

The truth is that everyone
is going to hurt you.

You just got to find the
ones worth suffering for.

The biggest challenge in life is to be yourself in a world that is trying to make your life like everyone else's.

If it does not burn a little,
then what's the point of
playing with fire?

Your soul shines when you
burn for your dreams.

Focus on the step-in front of you, not the whole staircase.

Accept both compliments and criticism. It takes both sun and rain for a flower to grow.

Don't practice until you get it right. Practice until you can't get it wrong."

Right now, your assignment is YOU. Water YOU

Logic will get you from point A to point B, imagination will take you everywhere.

Some people feel the rain,
others get wet.

Mirage By Aavriti

The nicest thing about rain
is that it stops. Eventually!

Do you need a reason to not
want to lose?

A person who never made a mistake, never tried anything new.

It's better to look
ahead and prepare than
to look back and regret.

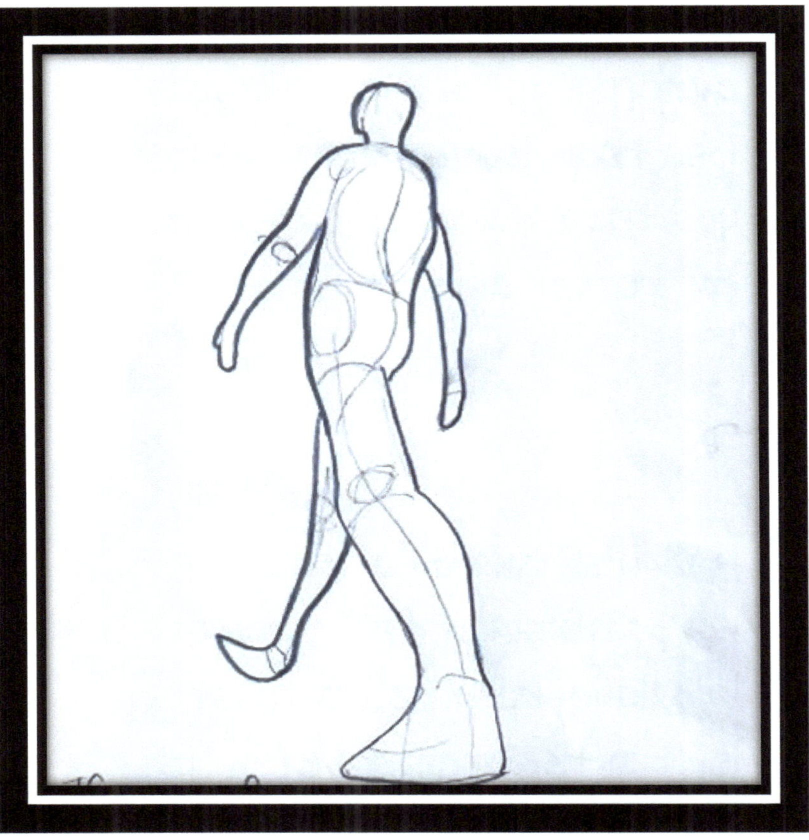

If you feel like you are losing everything, remember trees lose their leaves every year; yet they stand tall and wait for better days to come.

A bird sitting on a tree is never afraid of the branch breaking, because its trust isn't in the branch, but in its own wings.

The oceans don't apologize for their depth, nor do the mountains seek forgiveness for the space they take. So, neither should you.

Don't look for society to give you permission to be yourself.

Mirage By Aavriti

You get what you
WORK FOR and not
what you WISH for!!!

The one who falls
and gets up is so much
stronger that the one
who never fell.

Shine so bright that it
burns their eyes!

You have survived
too many storms to be
bothered by raindrops.

If one can do, you can do.

If none can do, you MUST do.

Strength doesn't come from lifting weights, it comes from lifting yourself every time you fall down.

DON'T raise your voice,
IMPROVE your argument!!!

Unity is POWER, but 100
sheep won't kill a wolf!!!

Be there for others, but
never leave yourself behind.

He who lives in harmony
with himself, lives in
harmony with the universe.

Be who you want to be, not what others want to see.

Mirage By Aavriti

Just because everyone is doing it doesn't make it right. Just because you are the only one doing it doesn't make it wrong.

Mirage By Aavriti

A dream means nothing if you don't grab it with your own hands.

Be yourself. People don't have to like you, and you don't have to care.

Bees don't waste their time explaining to flies that honey is better than shit.

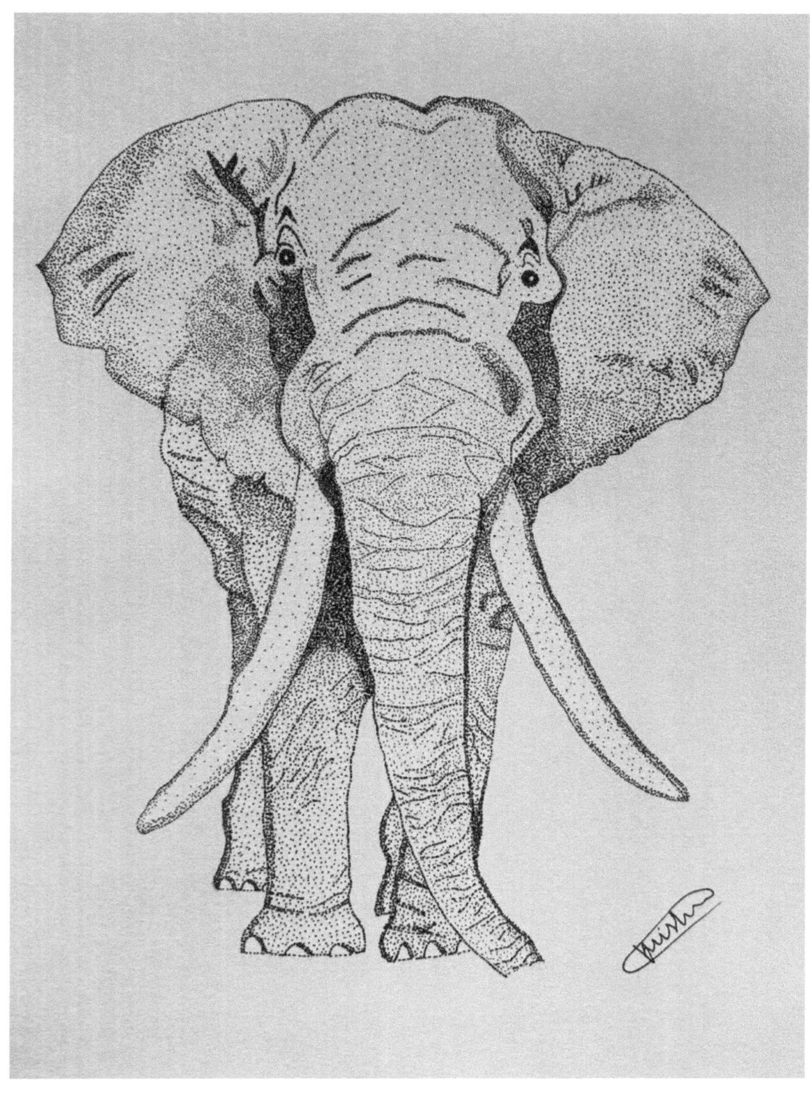

Go forth on your path, as it exists only through your walking.

Be who you want to be, not what others want to see.

The man who loves walking, will walk further than the man who loved the destination...

The moment you give up, is the moment you let someone else win...

Mirage By Aavriti

Raise your words, not your
voice.

It's the rain that grows
flowers; not thunder.

Focus on improving yourself,
not proving yourself.

Mirage By Aavriti

I would rather die on my feet than live on my knees.

Mirage By Aavriti

Sometimes it's not the people who change, it's the mask that falls off.

Be who you are and say what you feel because those who mind don't matter, and those who matter don't mind.

So, when you cursed a rose
that pricked your finger, just
remember the flower never
hides her barbs. It was your
haste to have her, before
you truly saw her, that left
a scar.

Nothing succeeds like success.

To succeed in life, you need 2 things: Ignorance and Confidence.

"It's impossible"; said Pride.

"It's risky"; said
Experience.

"It's pointless"; said
Reason.

"Give it a try"; whispered
the Heart.

If the plan doesn't wok, change the plan, not the goal.

Don't be afraid of being different, be afraid of being thesame as everyone else.

Sometimes we fall down because there is something down that we were supposed to find.

The game doesn't make sense if you don't aim to win.

Mirage By Aavriti

Whatever you are, be a
GOOD ONE!

Mirage By Aavriti

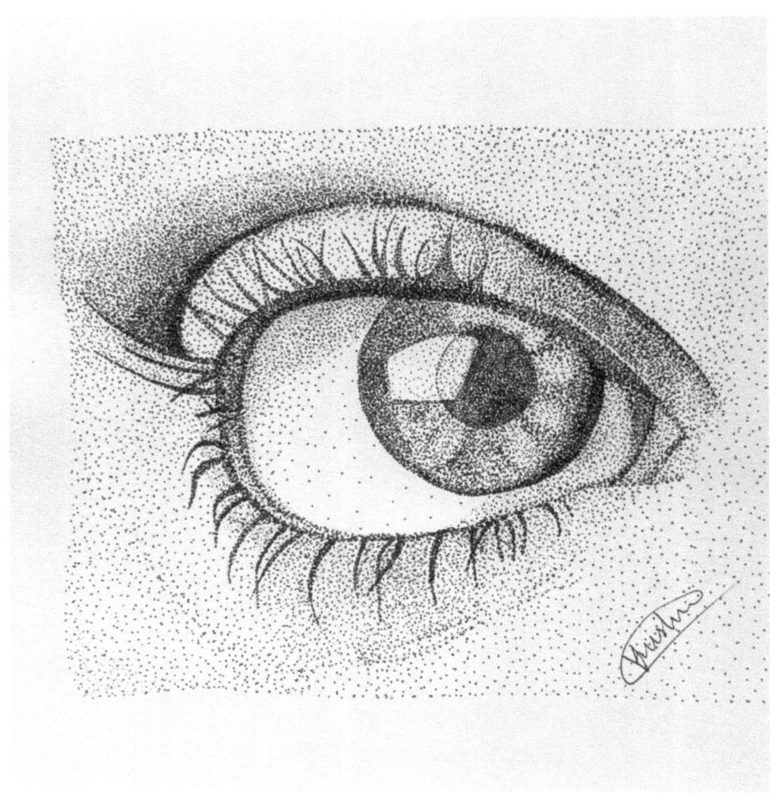

A brave human is the one who can look at the devils in the face and tell them they are devils.

If all you ever do is look down on people. You won't be able to recognize your own weakness.

Mirage By Aavriti

Hard work beats talent, when talent doesn't work hard.

Courage isn't having the strength to go on; it is going on when you don't have the strength.

Don't you think it's crazy that:

a millionaire won't judge you for starting a business.

a bodybuilder won't judge you for working.

an NBA player won't judge you for playing ball.

It's always those people who are going nowhere that want to judge you for trying to do something with your life.

The pain which gives you
wings is worth suffering.

Those who fly solo have the
strongest wings.

Mirage By Aavriti

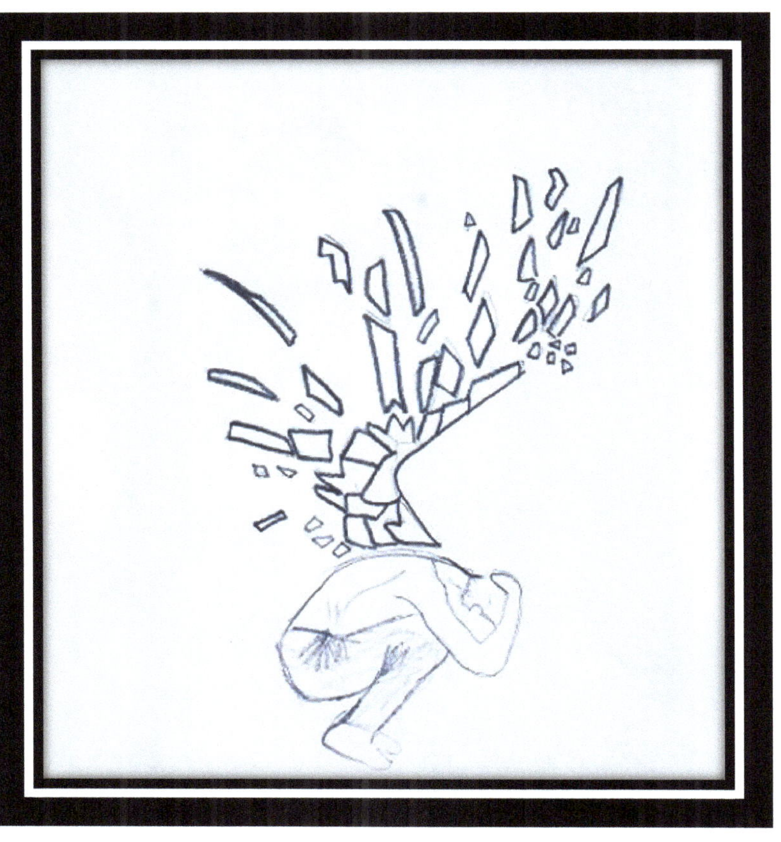

We are all in the same
game, just different levels.
Dealing with the same hell,
just different devils.

Sometimes it's not the
people who change, it's the
mask that falls off.

Mirage By Aavriti

Life isn't about finding yourself; it's about creating yourself.

Sometimes when you are invited....

..... You are still not welcome!!!

LEARN THE DIFFERENCE.

Real eyes, Realize, Real lies.

The day a blind man sees, the first thing he throws away is the stick that has helped him all his life.

You can't add days to your life, but you can add life to your days.

In the midst of where you are going, don't forget to enjoy where you are!

Either write things worth reading or do things worth writing.

It's fine to fight for someone who loves you, but it's a waste of time to fight for someone to love you.

Love yourself first and everything else falls into line.

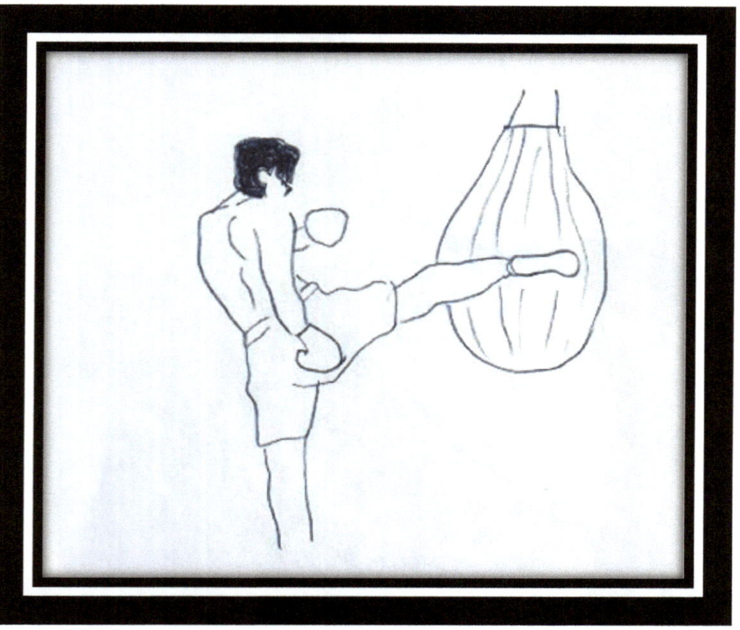

One day or Day 1? Your decide!

You have to be odd to be number 1!

It's on YOU, to get YOU, where YOU want to be.

There are 3 choices in life: Give In, Give Up or Give It Your All!

Happiness is
an inside job.
Don't assign
anyone else
that much
power in your
life!

Don't cross oceans
for people who wouldn't
cross a puddle for you.

And sometimes, against all odds, against all logic, WE HOPE.

As long as you don't give up, the possibility of winning will never fall to zero.

Mirage By Aavriti

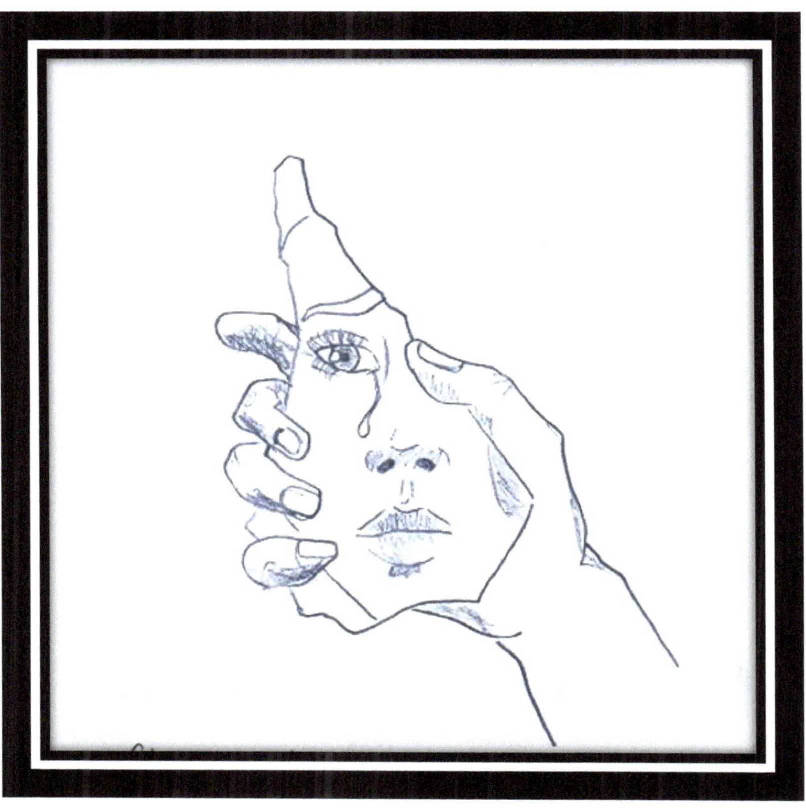

Glass needs to be
broken to be dangerous.

Either you run the day, or
the day runs you.

Mirage By Aavriti

The way people treat you,
is a statement about who
they are as a Human –
NOT ABOUT YOU!!!

Each time you reach a new
level,

Prepare yourself for a new
devil.

To fly, you will have to give up everything that weighs you down.

At school, we learn the lesson first before we get the test. But in life, we get the test first before we learn the lesson.

Just because my path is different, doesn't mean I'm lost.

The ones who say you can't, and you won't be probably the ones who are scared that you will.

Mirage By Aavriti

Be who you are and say what you feel, because those who mind don't matter and those who matter don't mind.

Mirage By Aavriti

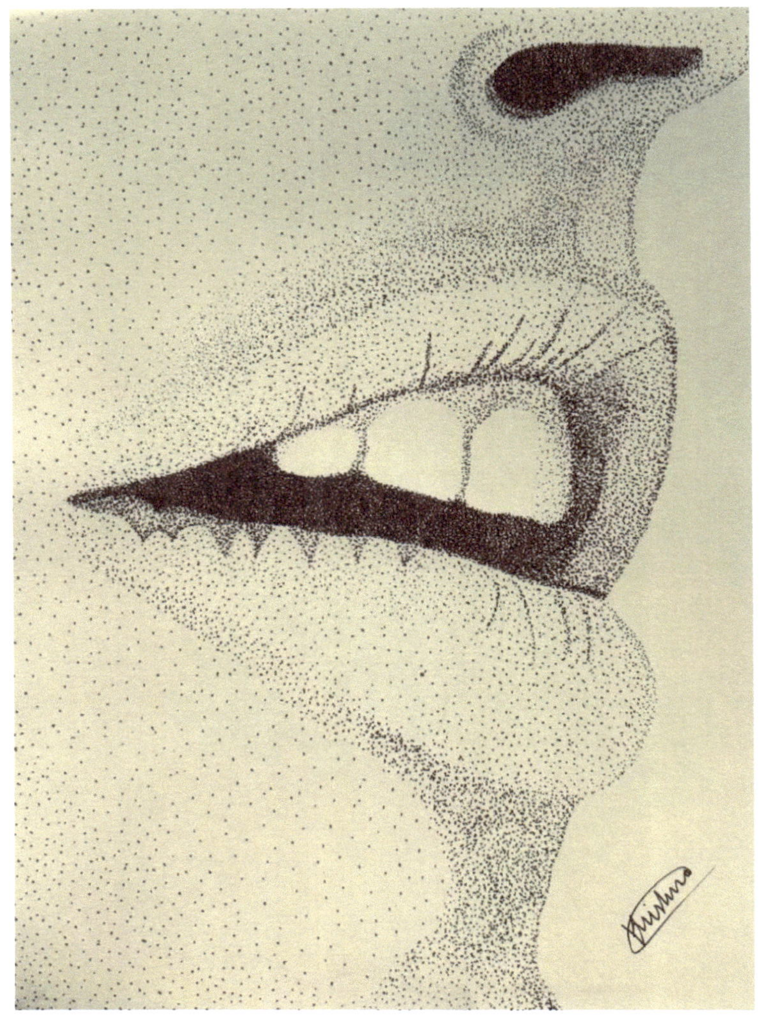

Only those people who
can dare to fail greatly, can
achieve greatly.

Be yourself, everyone else is
already taken.

We must not allow other
people's limited perceptions
to define us.

The ones who aren't able to
acknowledge themselves
are bound to fail.

Hurt people, hurt people.

The biggest risk in life is to not take any!!!

Don't cross oceans for people who wouldn't cross a puddle for you.

It's okay to outgrow people
who never grow.

You have survived too many storms to be bothered by raindrops.

Our hearts are monsters, that's why our ribs are cages.

Just because you love the
ocean doesn't mean you
have to drown in it.

The lion might be the king
of the jungle, but the wolf
never performs in a circus.

A writer is a world trapped
in a person.

Don't be too kind, this world
is too blind.

So, when you cursed a rose that pricked your finger, just remember the flower never hides her barbs. It was your haste to have her, before you truly saw her, that left a scar.

No one is perfect, that is
why pencils have erasers.

It shouldn't matter how
slowly a child learns, as long
as we are encouraging
them not to stop.

Home isn't where you are from. It's where you find light when everything grows dark.

The day you plant the seed isn't the day you eat the fruit.

Some people fear the fire. Some become it.

Children have never been very good at listening to their elders, but they have never failed to imitate them.

Allow children to be happy in their own way, for what better way will they find???

You can't control which
birds fly above your head,
but you can control which
one builds a nest over your
head.

The lion might be the king
of the jungle, but the wolf
never performs in a circus.

Some people fear the fire.
Some become it.

The most important thing in life, is knowing the most important things in life.

Nothing is IMPOSSIBLE,
the word itself says I M
POSSIBLE!!!

Slow down...

To

Run FAST!!!

"My mission in life is not merely to survive, but to thrive; and to do so with some passion, some compassion, some humour, and some style."

About the Author

Aavriti, a fun-loving, studious adventurer who enjoys painting, sketching, dancing and finding inspiration in quotes and stories. Though tech-savvy, she's channelled her online time positively: reading uplifting quotes, sketching online finds, and keeping positivity notes.

This book showcases her art and the quotes that fuel her. With this edition she hopes to inspire others to use their time positively and find their passion in things around them.

Hope you had fun reading and exploring the paintings and sketches.

You can reach out to Aavriti via her Instagram @Reetz_official.

Declaration

The book has quotes from some of the world leaders who inspired me while reading those and I wanted to share it with my family and friends. I hope this makes an impact and when you are feeling down, these give you the ray of light that I hope this book to provide.

The book has original sketches and paintings – some by me and some by my near and dear ones. There are sketches inspired by social media – which I found very interesting, inspiring and intriguing.

Thank you all for going through this book – which has been nothing short of my love for reading and drawing and making the most of the time that I get from the homeworks and the classworks.

What I am trying to do is....

Paint an inspiring picture

By

Tuning in the Meaningful Madness

9 798894 982830